Bootscooting

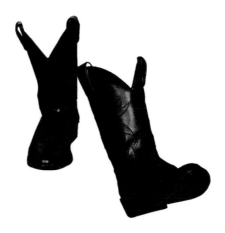

by Jill Brasell

photographs by Adrian Heke

Learning Media

I put on my shirt.

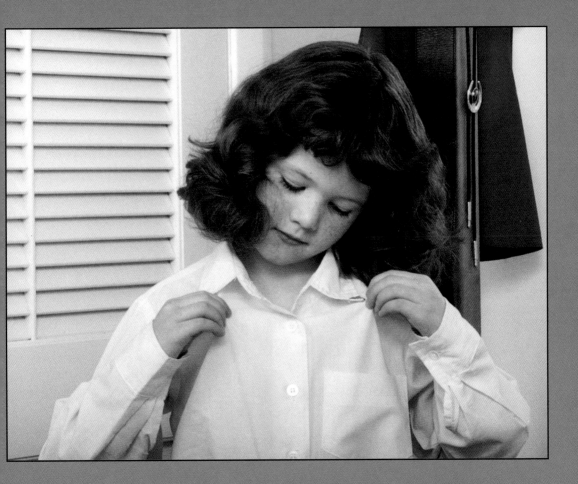

I put on my vest.

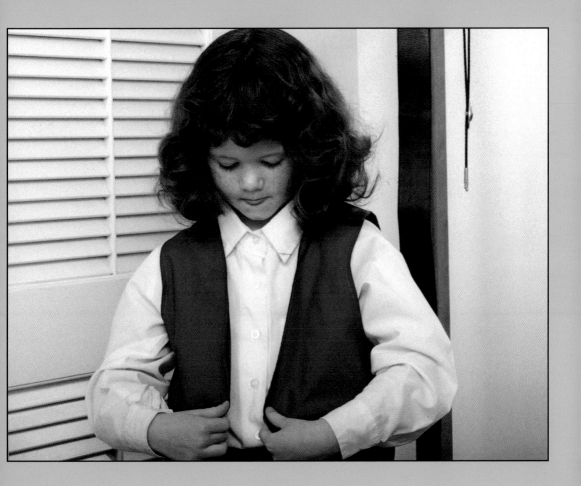

I put on my bolo.

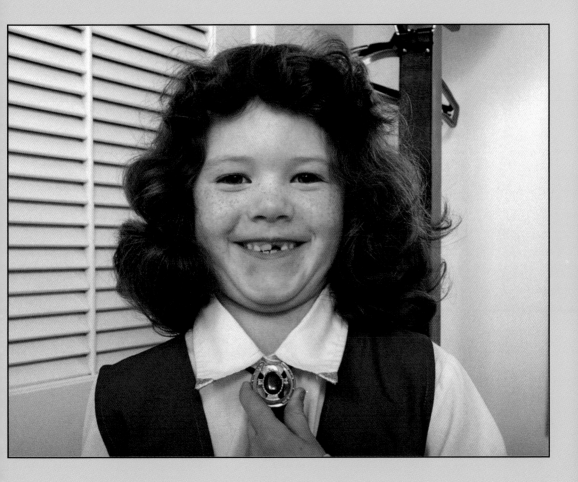

I put on my belt.

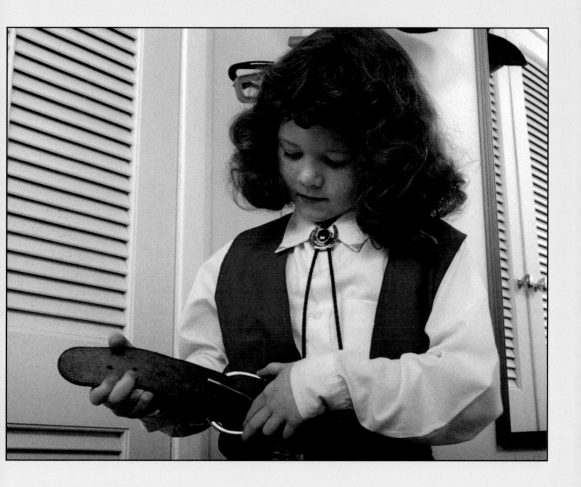

I put on my boots.

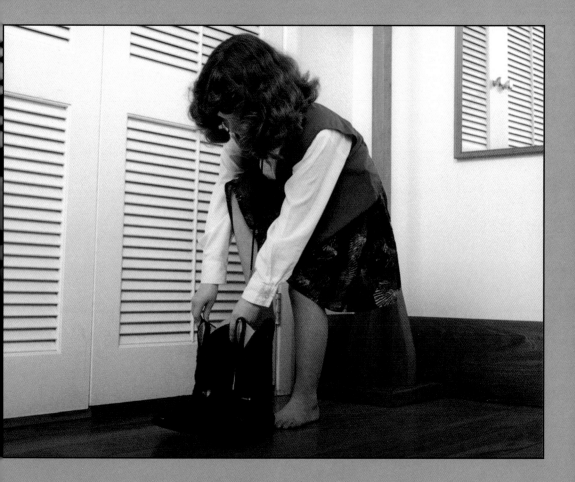

I put on my hat.

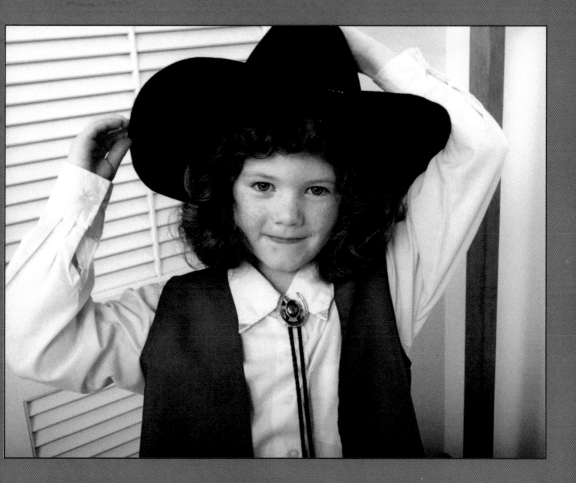

I put on my grin.

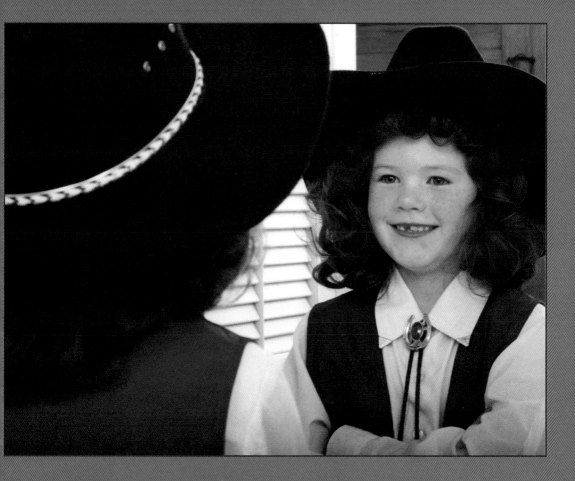

I go bootscooting.

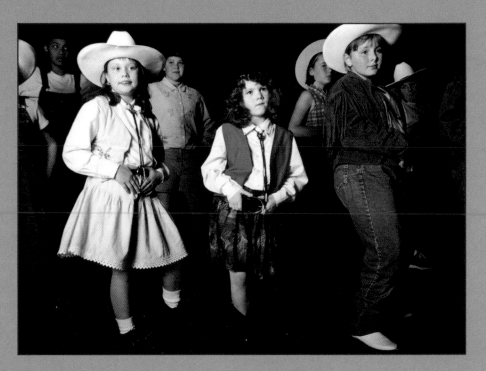